Dear Parent:
Your child's love of reading starts here!

Every child learns to read in a different way and at his or her own speed. Some go back and forth between reading levels and read favorite books again and again. Others read through each level in order. You can help your young reader improve and become more confident by encouraging his or her own interests and abilities. From books your child reads with you to the first books he or she reads alone, there are I Can Read Books for every stage of reading:

SHARED READING
Basic language, word repetition, and whimsical illustrations, ideal for sharing with your emergent reader

BEGINNING READING
Short sentences, familiar words, and simple concepts for children eager to read on their own

READING WITH HELP
Engaging stories, longer sentences, and language play for developing readers

READING ALONE
Complex plots, challenging vocabulary, and high-interest topics for the independent reader

ADVANCED READING
Short paragraphs, chapters, and exciting themes for the perfect bridge to chapter books

I Can Read Books have introduced children to the joy of reading since 1957. Featuring award-winning authors and illustrators and a fabulous cast of beloved characters, I Can Read Books set the standard for beginning readers.

A lifetime of discovery begins with the magical words **"I Can Read!"**

Visit www.icanread.com for information
on enriching your child's reading experience.

The Wildlife Conservation Society and Sharks

From 1930 to 1934, a Wildlife Conservation Society (WCS) scientist, William Beebe, was the first to explore the ocean's depths. In a bathysphere, an airtight sphere made of steel, he went three thousand feet beneath the ocean's surface and discovered many new kinds of animals.

Today, WCS continues to study and protect marine life, including sharks. WCS scientist Hans Walters works with sharks at the New York Aquarium and studies them in the wild. He attaches radio tags to sharks that record how far and how deep they swim. Organizations such as WCS work with governments all over the world to protect places where sharks live and breed.

At the New York Aquarium in Brooklyn, people can see sharks and other marine animals up close. To find out more about WCS and the ways you can help sharks and other endangered animals, visit www.wcs.org.

With gratitude to Peter Hamilton. Special thanks for photographs to Marty Snyderman, with the following exceptions: thanks to Brandon Cole (jacket front), Mote Marine Laboratory (pages 14–15), and Comstock Images, LLC (water background on pages 12-13).

Library of Congress Cataloging-in-Publication Data
Thomson, Sarah L.
   Amazing sharks! / written by Sarah L. Thomson ; photographs provided by the Wildlife Conservation Society.— 1st ed.
    p.   cm. — (An I can read book)
   ISBN-10: 0-06-054458-9 (trade bdg.) — ISBN-13: 978-0-06-054458-4 (trade bdg.)
   ISBN-10: 0-06-054457-0 (lib. bdg.) — ISBN-13: 978-0-06-054457-7 (lib. bdg.)
   ISBN-10: 0-06-054456-2 (pbk.) — ISBN-13: 978-0-06-054456-0 (pbk.)
   1. Sharks—Juvenile literature. I. Wildlife Conservation Society (New York, N.Y.) II. Title. III. Series.
QL638.9.T49 2005   2004022466
597.3—dc22   CIP
                                                                  AC

17 18 19 20 LSCC 30 29 28 27 26 25 24 23 22 21 20
❖

I Can Read!

READING
WITH HELP
2

AMAZING SHARKS!

WRITTEN BY
Sarah L. Thomson

PHOTOGRAPHS PROVIDED BY THE
Wildlife Conservation Society

 HarperCollins*Publishers*

 WILDLIFE CONSERVATION SOCIETY

There are more than 350

different kinds of sharks.

Some are as long as a fire truck.

Some are so small

you could hold one in your hand.

Some sharks have dull teeth.

Others have teeth so sharp

they can take a bite

out of a turtle's shell.

Some sharks live in rivers.

Others hide on the ocean bottom

or swim in deep water.

Some sharks even glow in the dark.

Almost all sharks are hunters.

Animals that hunt

are called predators.

(Say it like this: PRED-uh-tors.)

The white shark is a predator.

It attacks from below

to kill its favorite food—

seals or sea lions.

These animals are called its prey.

(It sounds the same as PRAY.)

A white shark can grow
as long as a pickup truck.
A whale shark can be as
long as two white sharks!
Its mouth can be wider
than your front door.

It is the biggest fish in the world.
But it eats mostly tiny animals
smaller than your fingernail.

The angel shark
hides under the sand
and waits for a fish to swim by.
Then the shark rushes out to eat it.

The cookie-cutter shark
takes just one bite out of a fish,
a whale, or a seal.
The bite is round, like a cookie.
Then the shark swims away.

angel shark

Sharks are fish,
but they are different
from other fish.
Other fish have bones.

A shark's skeleton is cartilage.

(Say it like this: CAR-til-idj.)

Your ears and nose

are made of cartilage.

It bends more easily than bone.

A shark can bend and twist

to turn quickly when it is swimming.

Most fish lay eggs in the water.

Some sharks lay eggs too.

But most sharks give birth

to their babies.

Shark babies are called pups.

The pups live on their own.

They do not need their parents.

They stay away from older sharks.

Some older sharks will eat pups

if they get the chance.

Some sharks eat stingrays

or spiny sea urchins.

Many eat other sharks.

Tiger sharks have eaten tin cans

and metal wire!

Sharks have rows

and rows of teeth.

If one tooth falls out,

a bigger one moves up

to fill in the hole.

Some sharks lose thousands of teeth

during their lives.

It can smell one drop of blood
in a million drops of water.

A shark can see well underwater.
A hammerhead shark has one eye
on each end of its long head.
No one is sure why.

If a fish is swimming or splashing,
a shark can feel the water moving.
Sharks can also feel electricity.

(Say it: EE-leck-TRIH-cih-tee.)

Every living thing gives off

a little bit of electricity.

People cannot feel it.

But sharks can.

Even if prey is hiding,

a shark can still find it

by feeling electricity in the water.

21

Many people are afraid of sharks.

But most sharks leave people alone.

You are more likely

to be hit by lightning

than to be killed by a shark.

People kill sharks every day.

They eat shark meat

or make their fins into soup.

They catch fish in huge nets.

Many sharks are killed by mistake

in these nets.

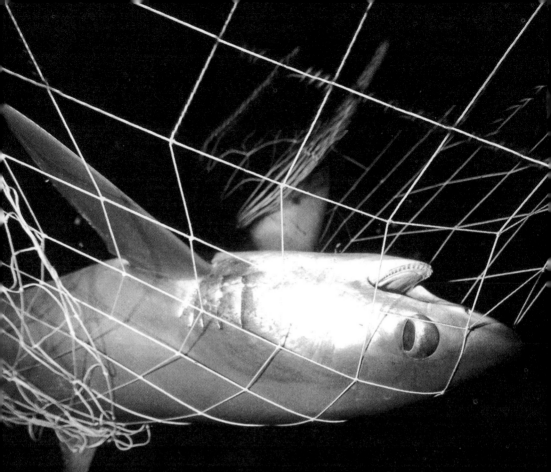

People have killed
more than half of all the sharks
in the world.

People dump trash or oil

into the ocean.

They put up buildings

near the shallow waters

where shark pups live and grow.

These waters are called nurseries.

If a nursery is destroyed,

pups may be eaten

by bigger fish or other sharks.

They will not grow up

and have pups of their own.

Scientists study sharks
to find out what they eat,
how far they swim,
how deep they dive,
and how many are still alive.
Sometimes they go into cages
under the water
so they can see sharks up close.
They learn how sharks live
and what they need to survive.

The ocean needs
predators like sharks.
Sharks hunt fish and other animals.
It is easiest for a shark
to catch a fish
that is weak or sick.
But strong and healthy
fish escape.

The fish lay eggs and have babies.

Their babies grow up

to be strong and healthy too.

Sharks are important
to life in the ocean.
People must find a way

to help sharks survive.

We can stop hunting sharks.

We can protect their nurseries.

We can teach other people
why we need
to have sharks
in our world.